EMMANUEL JOSEPH

The Art of Enough, Creativity, Compassion, and Decisions That Build a Better World

Copyright © 2025 by Emmanuel Joseph

All rights reserved. No part of this publication may be reproduced, stored or transmitted in any form or by any means, electronic, mechanical, photocopying, recording, scanning, or otherwise without written permission from the publisher. It is illegal to copy this book, post it to a website, or distribute it by any other means without permission.

First edition

This book was professionally typeset on Reedsy.
Find out more at reedsy.com

Contents

1. Chapter 1: Understanding "Enough" — 1
2. Chapter 2: The Power of Limitation — 3
3. Chapter 3: Cultivating Compassion — 5
4. Chapter 4: Redefining Success — 7
5. Chapter 5: Mindful Consumption — 9
6. Chapter 6: The Joy of Simplicity — 11
7. Chapter 7: Creative Problem Solving — 13
8. Chapter 8: Building Meaningful Relationships — 15
9. Chapter 9: Compassionate Leadership — 17
10. Chapter 10: Sustainable Living — 19
11. Chapter 11: Emotional Resilience — 21
12. Chapter 12: The Role of Community — 23
13. Chapter 13: Decision-Making with Integrity — 25
14. Chapter 14: The Intersection of Art and Enough — 27
15. Chapter 15: The Future of Enough — 29
16. Chapter 16: Personal Reflections — 31
17. Chapter 17: Taking Action — 33

1

Chapter 1: Understanding "Enough"

In a world driven by consumption and accumulation, the concept of "enough" can seem almost revolutionary. However, understanding what it means to have enough is essential for cultivating a fulfilling and sustainable life. The first step in this journey is to unravel the cultural, historical, and psychological factors that have shaped our perceptions of abundance and scarcity.

Historically, societies have evolved with the principle of more-is-better deeply ingrained in their ethos. From ancient civilizations that measured wealth by the size of their granaries to modern economies driven by consumerism, the idea of enough has often been overshadowed by the pursuit of excess. This relentless quest for more has had profound implications on our well-being and the environment. As we stand at the crossroads of unprecedented environmental and social challenges, it is imperative to reassess our values and redefine what it means to live well.

Psychologically, the fear of scarcity is a powerful motivator. Our brains are wired to seek security and abundance, a trait that has ensured human survival through millennia. However, in an era where basic needs are easily met for many, this instinct can drive us towards overconsumption and waste. By understanding the roots of these behaviors, we can begin to shift our mindset from one of scarcity to one of sufficiency, recognizing that having enough is not only adequate but also liberating.

The cultural narrative surrounding success is another key element in this equation. Success has often been measured by material possessions, social status, and financial wealth. This external validation can lead to a perpetual cycle of striving and dissatisfaction. However, redefining success on our own terms allows us to find contentment and purpose in ways that align with our values. It is a shift from external accumulation to internal fulfillment, from quantity to quality.

In this chapter, we will explore these themes in depth, providing a foundation for the transformative journey ahead. By embracing the concept of enough, we open ourselves to a life of greater creativity, compassion, and conscious decision-making. It is a journey that invites us to look within, to find peace in simplicity, and to build a better world through our choices.

2

Chapter 2: The Power of Limitation

While limitations are often perceived as obstacles, they can be powerful catalysts for creativity and innovation. When we embrace constraints, we force ourselves to think differently, to find solutions that we might not have considered in a world without boundaries.

One of the most profound examples of this is found in the world of art. Artists throughout history have often created their most iconic works under significant limitations—whether due to financial constraints, lack of materials, or societal restrictions. These challenges have driven them to experiment, to push the boundaries of their medium, and to develop unique styles that stand the test of time. By recognizing the potential within our limitations, we can tap into a wellspring of creativity that leads to innovative and meaningful outcomes.

In the realm of business and technology, limitations have similarly spurred breakthroughs. Startups with limited resources often innovate out of necessity, developing lean and efficient solutions that challenge established norms. The minimalist design philosophy, epitomized by companies like Apple, emphasizes the beauty and functionality that can emerge from simplicity and restraint. These examples illustrate how limitations, rather than stifling creativity, can actually enhance it by encouraging us to focus on what truly matters.

On a personal level, embracing limitations can lead to more mindful and intentional living. When we set boundaries on our time, energy, and resources, we are compelled to prioritize what is most important to us. This focus allows us to channel our efforts into pursuits that bring us joy and fulfillment, rather than dispersing our energy across a multitude of distractions. By appreciating the power of limitation, we cultivate a sense of gratitude for what we have and a deeper connection to our purpose.

This chapter delves into various examples and strategies for leveraging limitations to unlock our creative potential. It highlights the importance of shifting our perspective from viewing constraints as setbacks to recognizing them as opportunities for growth and innovation. By doing so, we not only enhance our own lives but also contribute to building a more resourceful and resilient world.

3

Chapter 3: Cultivating Compassion

At the heart of the art of enough lies compassion—the ability to understand and share the feelings of others. Compassion is more than an emotion; it is a practice that can transform our interactions and the world around us. By cultivating compassion, we create a foundation for a more harmonious and supportive society.

Compassion begins with empathy, the ability to put ourselves in someone else's shoes. This chapter explores the science behind empathy and its role in fostering compassionate behavior. It delves into the neurological and psychological mechanisms that enable us to connect with others' experiences and emotions. By understanding these processes, we can develop strategies to enhance our empathy and, in turn, our compassion.

Stories of individuals and communities who have embraced compassionate approaches offer powerful examples of the impact of empathy in action. From grassroots movements to global initiatives, these narratives showcase how compassion can lead to positive change. Whether it's supporting marginalized groups, advocating for social justice, or simply being present for a friend in need, compassionate actions ripple out to create a more inclusive and caring world.

Practicing compassion also involves self-compassion—being kind and understanding toward ourselves. This chapter highlights the importance of self-care and self-acceptance as essential components of a compassionate life. By treating ourselves with the same kindness we extend to others, we build emotional resilience and create a balanced foundation for fostering compassion externally.

Furthermore, the chapter discusses practical ways to cultivate compassion in our daily lives. It offers techniques for mindful listening, expressing empathy, and engaging in acts of kindness. These practices not only enhance our connections with others but also contribute to our overall well-being and happiness. By making compassion a central part of our interactions, we pave the way for a more empathetic and supportive society.

4

Chapter 4: Redefining Success

Success is a concept deeply ingrained in our collective consciousness, often measured by material wealth, social status, and professional achievements. However, this conventional definition of success can lead to a perpetual cycle of striving and dissatisfaction. To truly embrace the art of enough, we must redefine success in ways that align with our values and contribute to a better world.

This chapter challenges the traditional metrics of success and proposes alternative benchmarks that prioritize personal fulfillment and societal well-being. It explores the concept of intrinsic versus extrinsic goals—where intrinsic goals, such as personal growth, relationships, and meaningful contributions, lead to lasting satisfaction, while extrinsic goals, driven by external validation, often result in temporary fulfillment.

Redefining success involves shifting our focus from accumulation to contribution. This chapter highlights individuals and organizations that have embraced this mindset, finding success in their ability to make a positive impact rather than amass material wealth. It showcases stories of entrepreneurs, activists, artists, and everyday heroes who have redefined success by aligning their pursuits with their values and passions.

Moreover, the chapter provides practical strategies for redefining success in our own lives. It encourages readers to reflect on their personal goals and motivations, identifying what truly brings them joy and purpose. By setting intentions that align with our values, we create a roadmap for a fulfilling and meaningful life. This shift in perspective allows us to pursue goals that not only benefit ourselves but also contribute to the greater good.

Ultimately, redefining success is about finding balance—recognizing that having enough is not just about external achievements but also about internal contentment. By embracing this new definition, we can break free from the pressures of societal expectations and discover a more authentic and fulfilling way to live.

5

Chapter 5: Mindful Consumption

In a society driven by consumerism, embracing mindful consumption is a revolutionary act. Mindful consumption is about making conscious choices regarding what and how we consume, considering the broader impact on our well-being, society, and the environment. This chapter provides practical insights and strategies for adopting a more mindful approach to consumption.

Mindful consumption begins with awareness. It involves understanding the life cycle of the products we use—from production to disposal—and recognizing the environmental and social costs associated with them. This chapter explores the importance of being informed consumers, highlighting the need to consider factors such as sustainable sourcing, ethical labor practices, and eco-friendly packaging. By making informed choices, we can reduce our environmental footprint and support companies that align with our values.

Practical tips for mindful consumption include strategies for reducing waste, such as embracing a zero-waste lifestyle, opting for reusable products, and prioritizing quality over quantity. This chapter offers guidance on how to declutter our lives, both physically and mentally, to focus on what truly matters. By simplifying our consumption habits, we create space for experiences and relationships that bring us lasting joy and fulfillment.

Another essential aspect of mindful consumption is recognizing the impact of our choices on our mental and emotional well-being. This chapter discusses the phenomenon of retail therapy and how it often leads to temporary satisfaction followed by long-term dissatisfaction. By shifting our focus from acquiring material possessions to nurturing meaningful experiences and connections, we can cultivate a deeper sense of contentment.

Ultimately, mindful consumption is about finding balance. It is not about depriving ourselves but about making intentional choices that align with our values and contribute to a more sustainable and compassionate world. This chapter encourages readers to reflect on their consumption patterns and make small, manageable changes that collectively lead to significant positive impact.

6

Chapter 6: The Joy of Simplicity

Simplicity is often misconstrued as deprivation, but in reality, it is about finding joy in the essentials. Embracing simplicity allows us to focus on what truly matters, leading to a more fulfilling and peaceful life. This chapter delves into the beauty of simple living and offers practical insights for cultivating a lifestyle of intentional simplicity.

At its core, simplicity is about stripping away the excess to uncover the essence of what brings us joy and fulfillment. This chapter explores the philosophy of minimalism and its principles, such as intentionality, mindfulness, and the pursuit of meaningful experiences over material possessions. It highlights the benefits of decluttering both our physical spaces and our mental landscapes, allowing us to live with greater clarity and purpose.

The joy of simplicity is illustrated through stories of individuals who have embraced minimalist lifestyles. These narratives showcase the transformative power of simplicity, from reducing stress and anxiety to fostering creativity and personal growth. By letting go of the unnecessary, we create space for what truly enriches our lives.

Practical strategies for embracing simplicity include decluttering exercises, such as the KonMari method, and tips for organizing and maintaining a simplified living space. This chapter also discusses the importance of setting boundaries and saying no to commitments that do not align with our values. By prioritizing our time and energy, we can focus on activities and relationships that bring us genuine happiness.

Furthermore, the chapter highlights the connection between simplicity and sustainability. By consuming less and choosing quality over quantity, we reduce our environmental impact and contribute to a more sustainable world. Simplicity encourages us to live in harmony with nature, appreciating its beauty and resources without overexploiting them.

In essence, the joy of simplicity lies in discovering the richness of life through its most fundamental elements. By embracing simplicity, we can cultivate a sense of contentment and peace that transcends the pursuit of material wealth. This chapter invites readers to embark on a journey of intentional living, finding joy in the present moment and the essentials that truly matter.

7

Chapter 7: Creative Problem Solving

Creativity thrives when we recognize the sufficiency of our resources. Creative problem solving involves leveraging existing assets and thinking outside the box to find innovative solutions to challenges. This chapter explores techniques and strategies for fostering creativity through the art of enough.

One of the key principles of creative problem solving is the ability to see opportunities within limitations. This chapter discusses the concept of "frugal innovation," where constraints drive resourcefulness and ingenuity. It highlights examples from various fields, such as technology, business, and social entrepreneurship, where individuals and organizations have developed groundbreaking solutions with limited resources.

Techniques for creative problem solving include brainstorming, mind mapping, and design thinking. This chapter provides practical guidance on how to apply these methods to generate new ideas and address complex issues. It emphasizes the importance of a growth mindset—viewing challenges as opportunities for learning and development rather than obstacles.

The chapter also explores the role of collaboration in creative problem solving. By working together and pooling diverse perspectives, we can unlock collective creativity and develop more comprehensive solutions. It highlights the value of interdisciplinary collaboration and the power of diverse teams in driving innovation.

Furthermore, the chapter discusses the importance of experimentation and iteration in the creative process. It encourages readers to embrace a mindset of curiosity and openness, where failure is seen as a stepping stone to success. By iterating on ideas and learning from mistakes, we can refine our solutions and achieve greater impact.

Creative problem solving is not limited to professional or academic settings; it is a valuable skill in everyday life. This chapter provides examples of how individuals can apply creative thinking to personal challenges, such as time management, financial planning, and relationship building. By approaching problems with a mindset of enoughness, we can find innovative and sustainable solutions that enhance our well-being.

8

Chapter 8: Building Meaningful Relationships

Meaningful relationships are built on the foundation of mutual respect, understanding, and genuine connection. In a world where superficial interactions are common, cultivating deep and meaningful relationships requires intentionality and effort. This chapter explores how the art of enough fosters the development of authentic and lasting connections.

At the core of meaningful relationships is the practice of active listening and empathy. This chapter delves into the importance of truly hearing and understanding others, rather than merely waiting for our turn to speak. It provides techniques for improving active listening skills, such as maintaining eye contact, asking open-ended questions, and reflecting on what has been said. By being fully present in our interactions, we can build stronger and more genuine connections.

The chapter also highlights the value of quality over quantity in relationships. While having a large social network may seem desirable, the depth and authenticity of our connections are what truly matter. This chapter encourages readers to prioritize meaningful interactions with a few close friends and loved ones, rather than spreading themselves thin across numerous superficial relationships.

Building meaningful relationships also involves vulnerability and authenticity. This chapter discusses the importance of being open and honest with others, sharing our true selves rather than putting up façades. It explores the concept of emotional intimacy and how it strengthens bonds by fostering trust and mutual understanding.

Moreover, the chapter addresses the role of compassion and kindness in nurturing relationships. Acts of kindness, whether big or small, can have a profound impact on our connections with others. This chapter provides practical ideas for expressing compassion, such as offering support during difficult times, celebrating others' successes, and practicing forgiveness.

Finally, the chapter explores the significance of community and the sense of belonging it provides. It highlights stories of communities that have come together to support one another, creating a network of care and solidarity. By being active participants in our communities, we can build a sense of belonging and contribute to the well-being of those around us.

Meaningful relationships are a cornerstone of a fulfilling life. By embracing the principles of enough in our interactions, we can cultivate deep and lasting connections that enrich our lives and the lives of others.

9

Chapter 9: Compassionate Leadership

Leadership rooted in compassion has the potential to transform organizations and communities. Compassionate leaders prioritize the well-being of their team members, creating inclusive and supportive environments that foster collaboration and innovation. This chapter explores the qualities of compassionate leadership and its impact on building a better world.

Compassionate leadership begins with self-awareness and emotional intelligence. This chapter delves into the importance of understanding one's emotions and their influence on others. By cultivating self-awareness, leaders can navigate challenges with empathy and make decisions that consider the needs and perspectives of their team members. Emotional intelligence involves recognizing and managing emotions, both in oneself and in others, to foster positive interactions and relationships.

The chapter highlights the value of empathy in leadership. Compassionate leaders actively listen to their team members, seeking to understand their experiences, challenges, and aspirations. By demonstrating empathy, leaders create a culture of trust and respect, where individuals feel valued and supported. This chapter provides practical techniques for enhancing empathetic listening and communication skills, such as maintaining open body language, asking clarifying questions, and validating others' feelings.

Furthermore, the chapter discusses the role of vulnerability in compassionate leadership. By being open and authentic, leaders can build deeper connections with their team members and create a sense of psychological safety. Vulnerability fosters an environment where individuals feel comfortable sharing their ideas, taking risks, and learning from mistakes. This chapter explores the benefits of embracing vulnerability and provides strategies for cultivating authenticity in leadership.

Compassionate leadership also involves fostering a sense of purpose and meaning within the organization. This chapter highlights the importance of aligning organizational goals with values that prioritize social and environmental responsibility. By creating a shared vision that emphasizes making a positive impact, leaders can inspire and motivate their team members to contribute to a better world.

In essence, compassionate leadership is about creating a culture of care and collaboration. By prioritizing the well-being of others and leading with empathy and authenticity, leaders can build resilient and innovative organizations that thrive in a rapidly changing world.

10

Chapter 10: Sustainable Living

Sustainability is at the core of building a better world. Sustainable living involves making choices that minimize our environmental impact and promote the well-being of future generations. This chapter explores the principles of sustainable living and provides practical guidance for adopting sustainable practices in our daily lives.

At the heart of sustainable living is the recognition of our interconnectedness with nature. This chapter discusses the importance of understanding the environmental consequences of our actions and the need to live in harmony with the natural world. It highlights the principles of ecological footprint and carbon footprint, emphasizing the need to reduce our resource consumption and greenhouse gas emissions.

Practical strategies for sustainable living include reducing waste, conserving energy and water, and choosing sustainable transportation options. This chapter provides tips for implementing these practices, such as embracing a zero-waste lifestyle, using energy-efficient appliances, and opting for public transportation or cycling. By making small, manageable changes, we can collectively make a significant positive impact on the environment.

The chapter also explores the role of sustainable consumption in promoting environmental and social responsibility. It discusses the importance of choosing products that are ethically sourced, environmentally friendly, and produced by companies that prioritize sustainability. By supporting businesses that align with our values, we can drive positive change in the market and encourage more sustainable practices.

Furthermore, the chapter highlights the significance of community involvement in sustainability efforts. It showcases examples of communities that have come together to implement sustainable initiatives, such as community gardens, renewable energy projects, and local recycling programs. By working together, communities can create a collective impact that amplifies individual efforts and fosters a culture of sustainability.

Sustainable living is not just about reducing our environmental footprint; it is also about enhancing our quality of life. By embracing sustainable practices, we can improve our well-being, foster a sense of connection with nature, and contribute to a healthier and more resilient planet. This chapter encourages readers to reflect on their lifestyle choices and take actionable steps towards a more sustainable future.

11

Chapter 11: Emotional Resilience

Embracing enoughness fosters emotional resilience—the ability to navigate challenges and setbacks with strength and adaptability. Emotional resilience is essential for maintaining well-being and thriving in the face of adversity. This chapter explores strategies for building emotional resilience through the art of enough.

Emotional resilience begins with self-compassion. This chapter discusses the importance of being kind and understanding toward ourselves, especially during difficult times. By practicing self-compassion, we can soothe ourselves in moments of distress and build a foundation of inner strength. This chapter provides techniques for cultivating self-compassion, such as mindfulness meditation, positive self-talk, and self-care practices.

Another key aspect of emotional resilience is developing a growth mindset. This chapter explores the concept of viewing challenges as opportunities for learning and growth. By embracing a growth mindset, we can approach setbacks with curiosity and determination, rather than fear and frustration. Practical strategies for fostering a growth mindset include setting realistic goals, celebrating progress, and reframing negative thoughts.

The chapter also highlights the importance of building a support network. Strong relationships with family, friends, and community members provide a source of emotional support and encouragement. This chapter discusses the value of seeking help and sharing our experiences with others, as well as the benefits of offering support in return. By fostering meaningful connections, we can build a sense of belonging and resilience.

Furthermore, the chapter addresses the role of mindfulness in enhancing emotional resilience. Mindfulness involves being present and fully engaged in the moment, without judgment. This chapter provides practical exercises for incorporating mindfulness into daily life, such as mindful breathing, body scans, and mindful walking. By practicing mindfulness, we can develop greater emotional awareness and regulation, allowing us to respond to challenges with clarity and calmness.

Emotional resilience is not about avoiding difficulties but about navigating them with grace and strength. By embracing enoughness and cultivating resilience, we can thrive in the face of adversity and build a fulfilling and balanced life.

12

Chapter 12: The Role of Community

Communities thrive when members support and uplift each other. The art of enough fosters a sense of community by emphasizing collaboration, mutual aid, and collective well-being. This chapter explores the role of community in practicing enoughness and creating positive change.

At the heart of strong communities is the practice of mutual support. This chapter discusses the importance of helping one another and sharing resources, especially in times of need. It highlights examples of community initiatives, such as food banks, clothing drives, and neighborhood support groups, that provide assistance to those facing challenges. By fostering a culture of mutual aid, communities can create a safety net that ensures everyone has enough.

The chapter also explores the value of collaboration in building resilient communities. By working together, community members can pool their skills, knowledge, and resources to address common challenges. This chapter showcases stories of collaborative projects, such as community gardens, cooperative businesses, and local environmental initiatives, that have brought positive change to their neighborhoods. Collaboration fosters a sense of ownership and empowerment, allowing communities to take charge of their future.

Furthermore, the chapter highlights the importance of inclusivity and diversity in creating strong communities. Embracing diversity enriches the community by bringing together different perspectives, experiences, and talents. This chapter discusses strategies for promoting inclusivity, such as creating safe spaces for dialogue, celebrating cultural differences, and actively involving marginalized groups in community activities. By valuing and respecting diversity, communities can build a sense of belonging and unity.

The chapter also addresses the role of community in promoting well-being and mental health. Strong social connections and a sense of belonging are essential for emotional and psychological health. This chapter provides practical tips for building and maintaining meaningful relationships within the community, such as participating in local events, volunteering, and joining interest-based groups. By fostering a supportive and connected community, individuals can experience greater happiness and fulfillment.

In essence, the art of enough is not just an individual practice but a collective endeavor. By embracing the principles of enough within our communities, we can create a culture of care, collaboration, and resilience that benefits everyone.

13

Chapter 13: Decision-Making with Integrity

Making decisions aligned with our values is essential for personal fulfillment and societal well-being. Decision-making with integrity involves considering the broader impact of our choices and prioritizing compassion, creativity, and sustainability. This chapter offers frameworks for ethical decision-making and showcases examples of individuals and organizations leading with integrity.

At the core of ethical decision-making is the practice of aligning our actions with our values. This chapter discusses the importance of identifying and clarifying our core values, such as honesty, empathy, and responsibility. By using these values as a guiding compass, we can make decisions that reflect our commitment to a better world.

The chapter explores various ethical frameworks, such as consequentialism, deontology, and virtue ethics, providing practical guidance on how to apply these principles to real-life situations. It highlights the importance of considering the potential consequences of our actions, the duties we owe to others, and the virtues we wish to embody. By integrating these frameworks, we can navigate complex decisions with greater clarity and integrity.

Examples of ethical decision-making in action illustrate the impact of leading with integrity. This chapter features stories of individuals and organizations that have faced moral dilemmas and made choices that prioritize compassion, sustainability, and social justice. These narratives demonstrate the power of ethical leadership in driving positive change and inspiring others to follow suit.

Practical strategies for ethical decision-making include techniques for critical thinking, such as analyzing potential outcomes, seeking diverse perspectives, and reflecting on past experiences. This chapter also discusses the importance of transparency and accountability in decision-making processes. By being open and honest about our choices and their rationales, we build trust and credibility with others.

Decision-making with integrity is not about perfection but about striving to do the right thing to the best of our abilities. By embracing ethical decision-making, we contribute to a culture of integrity and compassion that benefits both individuals and society as a whole.

14

Chapter 14: The Intersection of Art and Enough

Art has the power to inspire and provoke change, making it a powerful medium for communicating the message of enoughness. This chapter explores how artists use their craft to challenge societal norms and encourage viewers to rethink their perceptions of abundance and scarcity.

Artistic expression often emerges from a place of limitation and resourcefulness. This chapter discusses how artists leverage the concept of enough to create impactful works that resonate with audiences. It highlights examples of art created from reclaimed materials, minimalist designs, and thought-provoking installations that invite viewers to reflect on their own consumption patterns.

The chapter also explores the role of storytelling in art. Through narratives, artists can convey the emotional and social dimensions of enoughness, making abstract concepts more tangible and relatable. This chapter features stories of artists who have used their work to advocate for environmental sustainability, social justice, and compassionate living. By telling stories that resonate with people's experiences, artists can inspire action and foster a deeper understanding of the art of enough.

Furthermore, the chapter delves into the collaborative nature of art. Many artists work in communities, engaging with others to create collective works that reflect shared values and aspirations. This chapter showcases examples of community art projects that bring people together to explore themes of enoughness and sustainability. Through collaboration, art becomes a powerful tool for building connections and fostering a sense of belonging.

The intersection of art and enough is also evident in the movement towards slow art and mindful creation. This chapter discusses the importance of intentionality in the creative process, emphasizing the value of quality over quantity. It highlights the work of artists who prioritize sustainability in their materials and methods, creating pieces that embody the principles of enoughness.

Art has the potential to challenge, inspire, and transform. By exploring the intersection of art and enough, we can appreciate the profound impact of creativity in shaping a more compassionate and sustainable world.

15

Chapter 15: The Future of Enough

As we look to the future, the concept of enough has the potential to shape a more sustainable and just world. This chapter discusses emerging trends and movements that embrace enoughness and envision a future where creativity, compassion, and mindful decision-making are at the forefront of progress.

One of the key trends is the growing emphasis on sustainability and environmental stewardship. This chapter explores how individuals, businesses, and governments are increasingly prioritizing sustainable practices to address climate change and preserve natural resources. It highlights initiatives such as the circular economy, renewable energy adoption, and regenerative agriculture that embody the principles of enough.

The chapter also discusses the rise of social innovation and the shift towards purpose-driven business models. Entrepreneurs and organizations are increasingly recognizing the importance of creating value beyond profit, focusing on social and environmental impact. This chapter features examples of businesses that have integrated enoughness into their core values, demonstrating how profitability and sustainability can go hand in hand.

Furthermore, the chapter explores the role of education in fostering a mindset of enough. As awareness of environmental and social issues grows, educational institutions are incorporating sustainability and ethics into their curricula. This chapter highlights programs and initiatives that empower students to think critically about their consumption patterns and make informed, ethical decisions. By nurturing a new generation of compassionate and mindful leaders, we can build a future grounded in the principles of enough.

The future of enough also involves reimagining our relationship with technology. While technology has the potential to exacerbate overconsumption, it also offers innovative solutions for promoting sustainability and well-being. This chapter discusses how advancements in technology, such as smart cities, sustainable design, and digital platforms for sharing resources, can support the transition to a more sustainable and just world.

In essence, the future of enough is about embracing a holistic approach to progress—one that values creativity, compassion, and mindful decision-making. By envisioning and working towards a future grounded in enoughness, we can create a world that prioritizes well-being, resilience, and harmony with nature.

16

Chapter 16: Personal Reflections

Personal stories and reflections bring the abstract concept of enough to life. This chapter features accounts from individuals who have embraced enoughness in their lives, providing inspiration and practical insights for readers to apply in their own journeys.

The chapter begins with stories of individuals who have simplified their lives and found greater fulfillment. These narratives highlight the transformative power of minimalism and intentional living, showcasing how letting go of excess can lead to greater clarity, peace, and joy. By sharing their experiences, these individuals offer practical tips for decluttering, prioritizing, and finding contentment in simplicity.

The chapter also includes reflections on the role of compassion in personal transformation. Individuals who have adopted practices of empathy and kindness share how these principles have enriched their relationships and overall well-being. Their stories emphasize the importance of self-compassion and the impact of extending compassion to others, providing readers with insights on how to cultivate a more compassionate and connected life.

Additionally, the chapter features accounts of individuals who have made conscious choices to align their actions with their values. These stories illustrate the significance of ethical decision-making and the fulfillment that comes from living with integrity. By sharing their journeys, these individuals inspire readers to reflect on their own values and make choices that contribute to a better world.

Personal reflections on sustainable living are also highlighted in this chapter. Individuals who have adopted eco-friendly practices share their experiences of reducing waste, conserving resources, and living in harmony with nature. Their stories provide practical guidance on how to integrate sustainability into daily life and emphasize the interconnectedness of personal choices and global outcomes.

Ultimately, personal reflections offer a window into the lived experiences of embracing enough. By sharing these stories, this chapter aims to inspire readers to embark on their own journeys of enoughness, discovering the transformative power of creativity, compassion, and mindful decision-making.

17

Chapter 17: Taking Action

The final chapter is a call to action, encouraging readers to take concrete steps towards practicing the art of enough. By integrating the principles discussed throughout the book into everyday life, readers can contribute to building a more creative, compassionate, and sustainable world.

The chapter begins with practical tips for incorporating the concept of enough into daily routines. It offers strategies for mindful consumption, such as evaluating needs versus wants, choosing quality over quantity, and supporting ethical and sustainable brands. By making intentional choices, readers can reduce their environmental impact and align their consumption patterns with their values.

The chapter also provides guidance on cultivating creativity and innovation within the framework of enough. It encourages readers to embrace limitations as opportunities for growth, experiment with new ideas, and seek out collaborative opportunities. By fostering a mindset of resourcefulness and creativity, readers can develop innovative solutions to personal and collective challenges.

Furthermore, the chapter emphasizes the importance of compassion in creating a better world. It offers practical suggestions for practicing empathy and kindness, such as volunteering, supporting community initiatives, and advocating for social justice. By extending compassion to others and ourselves, readers can build stronger connections and contribute to a more inclusive and supportive society.

The chapter also highlights the significance of ethical decision-making and integrity. It encourages readers to reflect on their values and consider the broader impact of their choices. By prioritizing actions that align with their principles, readers can lead with integrity and inspire others to do the same.

Finally, the chapter discusses the importance of community involvement and collective action. It encourages readers to actively participate in their communities, support local initiatives, and collaborate with others to create positive change. By working together, we can amplify our individual efforts and build a culture of enough that benefits everyone.

The Art of Enough: Creativity, Compassion, and Decisions That Build a Better World

In a world that often equates success with accumulation, "The Art of Enough" presents a transformative approach to living well through the principles of creativity, compassion, and mindful decision-making. This enlightening book invites readers to explore the profound impact of embracing enoughness, not just as a philosophy, but as a practical way of life.

With chapters that delve into the power of limitations, the joy of simplicity, and the importance of ethical decision-making, "The Art of Enough" offers a roadmap for finding balance and fulfillment. Through personal reflections, inspiring stories, and actionable strategies, readers will discover how to foster creativity within constraints, build meaningful relationships, and lead with compassion and integrity.

From mindful consumption to sustainable living, this book provides practical insights for reducing our environmental footprint and living in harmony with nature. It also emphasizes the significance of community and collective action in creating positive change, showcasing how small, intentional choices can lead to a more compassionate and sustainable world.

"The Art of Enough" challenges conventional metrics of success and proposes a new definition that prioritizes personal growth, well-being, and social impact. By redefining success and embracing the art of enough, readers are empowered to make choices that align with their values and contribute

CHAPTER 17: TAKING ACTION

to a better world.

This book is a call to action for anyone seeking a more intentional and fulfilling life. It offers a fresh perspective on what it means to have enough and provides the tools to cultivate a life of creativity, compassion, and conscious decision-making. Embark on this journey of enoughness and discover the joy and peace that come from living in alignment with your true values.

www.ingramcontent.com/pod-product-compliance
Lightning Source LLC
LaVergne TN
LVHW020458080526
838202LV00057B/6026